DESTINATION
Middle Ages

Your Guide to the
Islamic
Golden Age

Tim Cooke

Crabtree Publishing Company
www.crabtreebooks.com

Crabtree Publishing Company

www.crabtreebooks.com

Author: Tim Cooke

Designer: Lynne Lennon

Picture Manager: Sophie Mortimer

Design Manager: Keith Davis

Editorial Director: Lindsey Lowe

Children's Publisher: Anne O'Daly

Editor: Petrice Custance

Proofreader: Wendy Scavuzzo

**Production coordinator
and prepress technician:** Tammy McGarr

Print coordinator: Margaret Amy Salter

Written and produced for Crabtree Publishing Company
by Brown Bear Books

Photographs (t=top, b=bottom, l=left, r=right, c=center):
Front Cover: Dreamstime: Eduard Kim tr; **Jacopo:** br;
Public Domain: cr; **Topkapi Palace Museum:** main.

Interior: 123rf: 12, 18r; **Alamy:** Lanmas 15t, Mary Evans Picture Library 28, Print Collector 16bl, Prisma Archivo 22r; **Bluemangoa:** 24t; **Bridgeman Art Library:** Ashmolean Museum 15b, San Diego Museum of Art 11b; **Fabrizio Castello:** Orazio Cambiasco, Lazzaro Tavarone (and Ian Pitchford) 29t; **Dreamstime:** Eduard Kim 18bl; **Escurial Library:** 26r; **James Gordon:** 26bl; **Metropolitan Museum of Art:** 20tr; **Musée du Louvre:** 24br; **Palace of Versailles:** 10b; **Public Domain:** 5t, 29tr, Everipedia 17, WikiVisually 25br; **Shutterstock:** 13b, 14, 23l, Toni Genes 9t, Trevor Kittelty 27r, Mikail Markovskiy 10tl, Dejan Stanisavijevic 23b, Luisma Tapia 8; Prakash Subbarao 19t; **SuperStock:** Weapon and Warfare 16r; **Thinkstock:** istockphoto 19b, 22bl, 25t, Photos.com 5b; **Topfoto:** Granger Collection 9b, 11t; **travelogues gr/collection:** 13t; **Victoria and Albert Museum:** 27bl; **Walters Art Museum:** Acquired by Henry Walters 4; **Wellcome Library:** Wellcome Images 20bl, 21. All other photos, artwork and maps, **Brown Bear Books**.

Brown Bear Books has made every attempt to contact the copyright holder. If you have any information please contact licensing@brownbearbooks.co.uk

Library and Archives Canada Cataloguing in Publication

Cooke, Tim, 1961-, author
        Your guide to the Islamic Golden Age / Tim Cooke.

(Destination: Middle Ages)
Includes index.
Issued in print and electronic formats.
ISBN 978-0-7787-2993-8 (hardcover).--
ISBN 978-0-7787-2999-0 (softcover).--
ISBN 978-1-4271-1866-0 (HTML)

        1. Islamic Empire--History--Juvenile literature. 2. Islamic civilization--History--Juvenile literature. 3. Middle Ages--Juvenile literature. I. Title.

DS36.85.C67 2017   j909'.0976701   C2016-907395-5
                                                                 C2016-907396-3

Library of Congress Cataloging-in-Publication Data

Names: Cooke, Tim (Writer on Islamic history), author.
Title: Your guide to the Islamic golden age / Tim Cooke.
Description: New York, N.Y. : Crabtree Publishing Company, [2017] |
    Series: Destination: Middle Ages | Includes index.
Identifiers: LCCN 2016055839 (print) | LCCN 2016057660 (ebook) |
    ISBN 9780778729938 (reinforced library binding : alk. paper) |
    ISBN 9780778729990 (pbk. : alk. paper) |
    ISBN 9781427118660 (Electronic HTML)
Subjects: LCSH: Islam--History--Juvenile literature. | Islamic Empire--History--Juvenile literature. | Islamic civilization--Juvenile literature.
Classification: LCC BP55 .C665 2017 (print) | LCC BP55 (ebook) |
    DDC 909/.09767--dc23
LC record available at https://lccn.loc.gov/2016055839

Crabtree Publishing Company

www.crabtreebooks.com   1-800-387-7650

Printed in Canada/032017/BF20170111

Published in Canada
Crabtree Publishing
616 Welland Ave.
St. Catharines, ON
L2M 5V6

Published in the United States
Crabtree Publishing
PMB 59051
350 Fifth Avenue, 59th Floor
New York, New York 10118

Published in the United Kingdom
Crabtree Publishing
Maritime House
Basin Road North, Hove
BN41 1WR

Published in Australia
Crabtree Publishing
3 Charles Street
Coburg North
VIC, 3058

Contents

Before We Start

In Arabia in the 600s, a man named Muhammad believed God spoke to him. What he heard would change the world forever.

A GOLDEN AGE

+ Islam reaches a peak

Historians use the term "golden age" to describe a time of peace, prosperity, and great **cultural** advances. In the Islamic world, the golden age is usually dated from the 700s to the 1200s. At that time, Islamic **caliphs** ruled over an empire that covered much of the Middle East, North Africa, and Central Asia. These rulers encouraged international trade and commissioned scholars to study **astronomy**, math, and medicine, while artists and architects created great works.

LIFE OF THE PROPHET

+ Muhammad preaches the new faith

+ Flees from his home

Muhammad was born in Mecca in Arabia around 570. At the age of 40, he began to hear God's words. He started to preach, and gained many followers. His enemies forced him to flee Mecca in 622 and he moved to Medina. He later returned, and established a **mosque** in Mecca (shown on this painted tile, right). By the time of his death in 632, Muhammad's teachings were the basis of a new religion, called Islam.

> *Allah [God] did not send me to be harsh or cause harm, but he sent me to teach and make things easy.*

The Prophet Muhammad

ISLAM SPREADS

✦ **From Arabia across the world...**

✦ **...warriors carry the faith**

By 630, Muhammad had united the tribes of Arabia under his new religion. After his death two years later, his followers converted people to Islam throughout the Middle East. Arab warriors fought many wars to spread the religion (below). By 732, Islam had spread through Persia to India, along Africa's north coast, and into southern Spain.

ISLAM DIVIDED

✦ **Muslim vs Muslim**

✦ **Split continues today**

When Muhammad died, his followers split into two groups. The larger group were the Sunnis. They wanted Muhammad's friend Abu Bakr to become caliph. The Shia, on the other hand, wanted Muhammad's cousin and son-in-law Ali to become caliph. In fact, Abu Bakr became the first caliph. Ali later became the fourth caliph. The split between the Sunnis and the Shia continues today.

LIGHT IN THE DARK AGES

☛ **A scholarly culture**

Islam was based on learning. Islamic scholars studied texts by ancient Greek thinkers such as Aristotle (left) and Plato. Meanwhile, Europe was in a period known as the "Dark Ages." Learning collapsed as tribes fought each other. It was only thanks to Islamic scholars that many texts from the **classical** world were preserved.

Where in the World?

By 732, the Islamic Empire had spread from the Indian border in the east to Spain and Portugal, known as Andalusia, in the west.

Cordoba
From 929 to 1031, Cordoba was the capital of the Umayyad **dynasty**, who ruled much of Spain and North Africa. Cordoba was famous as a center of scholarship.

Cairo
The Arab Fatimid caliphs founded Cairo in 969 and it became their capital in 1169. In 1250, the city was seized by slave soldiers called Mamluks, whose dynasty ruled it until 1517.

Mecca and Medina
The Prophet Muhammad founded Islam in Mecca, and it remains the holiest site for all Muslims. When local people objected to the new faith, Muhammad took shelter in Medina, which is also a holy city in Islam. He later returned to Mecca.

RUSSIA

EUROPE

SPAIN

PORTUGAL

Cordoba

TUNISIA

AFRICA

SYRIA

Damascus

Jerusalem

Cairo

EGYPT

Medina

Mecca

Damascus

Damascus in Syria was the capital of the Umayyad **Caliphate** from 661 to 750. The Umayyads made Arabic the official language, even though most citizens of Damascus were Christians who did not speak Arabic.

Jerusalem

Jerusalem is holy to Muslims, Christians, and Jews. Muslim armies seized the city from the Byzantine Empire in 637. In the Crusades that began in 1095, European Christians fought a series of campaigns to try to win the city back.

Baghdad

Baghdad was founded by the Abbasid dynasty as their capital in the mid-700s. It was the capital of the Arab Caliphate during the golden age of the 800s and 900s, when it was the largest city in the world. Baghdad was a trade center, and a renowned center of learning and Islamic culture.

IRAQ

IRAN   AFGHANISTAN

Baghdad

SAUDI
ARABIA

INDIA

Arabia

Arabia is a large peninsula between Asia and Africa. It is bordered on one side by the Persian Gulf and on the other by the Red Sea. This desert region was home to the Islamic religion.

New Names

This map shows the modern names of the countries that were part of the Islamic Empire at its height.

Who We'll Meet

Many outstanding people contributed to the Islamic Golden Age. They ranged from rulers to great thinkers and poets, and also included women whose contributions are often overlooked.

ABBASID RULER

✦ Living in luxury

✦ Glory days in Baghdad

Harun al-Rashid was the fifth caliph of the Abbasid dynasty. He ruled from Baghdad at the end of the 700s. Al-Rashid used taxes to pay for outstanding new buildings in the city and to commission other artistic works. The Abbasid court was famed for its luxury.

WOMEN'S ROLES

✦ Spreading the faith...

✦ ...supporting education

It was unusual for women to have roles outside the home, but some women had key roles in the Golden Age. Fatima Al-Fihri, for example, built the Qarawiyyin Mosque and University in Fes, Morocco, in 859. In the 900s, Sutayta Al-Mahamali was a skilled mathematician, while three centuries later Zaynab Al Shahda was famed for her **calligraphy**, or artistic handwriting.

INFLUENTIAL PHILOSOPHER

+ It might all be Greek...

+ ...but Ibn Rushd explained it

Ibn Rushd, also known as Averroes, was an Islamic scholar who lived in Cordoba in Spain in the 1100s. Ibn Rushd studied the works of the Greek **philosophers** Plato and Aristotle. He wrote explanations of their ideas about politics and the law. His studies were influential, not just in the Islamic world, but also in Europe.

A JEWISH INTELLECTUAL

☛ **Maimonides is super smart**

Moses Maimonides lived in the 1100s. He was a leading Jewish thinker who lived and worked in Cordoba, Spain. Although Cordoba was a Muslim city, it had a large population of Jews. Maimonides studied philosophy, law, and medicine, and wrote books in Hebrew and Arabic. His writings were widely read.

Did you know?

Rumi's poems are still popular. He is the best-selling poet in the United States today. His poems address subjects such as love, life, and happiness.

BREAKING NEWS

A preacher in Persia is making a name for his poetry. Rumi (right) was a wealthy religious teacher before he met a wandering holy man who persuaded him to change. Rumi is now a Sufi, or **mystic**, and has written about 30,000 poems. They are often about **spiritual** subjects, such as his relationship with God. They are not strictly Islamic, however. Rumi's poems look likely to have a wide appeal to Christians and others.

A Little Bit of History

Inspired by the belief that they were doing God's work, Muhammad's followers were eager to spread the Islamic faith. Eventually, the Muslim Empire stretched from Spain to India.

THE HOLY CITY

- ✦ **Everyone claims Jerusalem**
- ✦ **Home to sacred sites**

Jerusalem is **sacred** to three religions: Islam, Judaism, and Christianity. Muslims conquered the city in the 600s and lived peacefully there with Jews and Christians for about 400 years. The city contains the Temple Mount complex, which includes some of Islam's holiest sites, such as the Dome of the Rock (left) and the Al-Aqsa mosque.

HOLY WARS!

- + **Christians launch Crusades**
- + **Islamic armies hit back**

In the 1000s, Christian **pilgrims** complained about the difficulty of traveling to Jerusalem through Turkey. The Christian Byzantine Empire, based in Constantinople, was at war with the Muslim Seljuk Turks. Europeans launched a new series of wars against the Muslims. These so-called **Crusades** (right) aimed to take control of Jerusalem and the Holy Land. The Christian campaigns had little success.

ABBASID BAGHDAD

+ **City reaches new heights**
+ **Inspires cultural explosion**

Under the seventh Abbasid caliph, Al-Mamun (right), Baghdad was the most important city in the world. Between 813 and 833, the city was the center of Islamic scholarship. The focus of this boom was the House of Wisdom, a center where scholars from across the world came to study and teach.

On Crusade

In 1095, Pope Urban II, head of the Roman Catholic Church, told European Christians it was their duty to fight Muslims in the Holy Land.

NEWS FROM AFAR

From Arabia, Islam spread through the Middle East, North Africa, southern Spain, India, and Indonesia. It reached as far east as China. Different dynasties held regional power, including the Abbasids of Persia and the Ottomans of present-day Turkey.

A NEW ISLAMIC POWER

☞ **Osman founds an empire**

☞ **Ottomans capture Turkey**

The Ottomans were **nomads** from Central Asia. Under their leader Osman (right), they settled in Turkey in the late 1200s. Their army conquered a large empire. In the 1400s and 1500s, the Ottoman Empire was one of the world's most powerful states. Its capital, Constantinople, was famed for its beautiful buildings. The Ottoman Empire lasted more than 600 years, until 1922.

The Islamic World

As the Islamic Empire expanded, it took in different nationalities with their own culture. The caliph appointed governors to rule each region on his behalf.

The Mosque

At the heart of a Muslim city was the mosque. A **muezzin** called Muslims to prayer five times a day from the mosque's **minaret**, a high tower.

THE CALIPH

+ **Head of the faith**

+ **Spiritual leader**

After Muhammad died in 632, Muslim leaders chose Abu Bakr as his successor. He became the first caliph (*khalifa*), which means "successor" or "**viceroy**." The caliph's duty was to rule all Muslims according to Islamic ideas. He was also the head of the army. As the empire grew, the caliph relied on Muslim leaders known as **sultans** to govern different parts of the empire.

THE ISLAMIC WORLD TODAY

✦ **Lure of the caliphate**

Under the Ottoman Turks, the Islamic caliphate grew weak over centuries. In 1924, it was abolished. Since then, many groups have called for a new caliphate to rule the Muslim world. The most recent are the **terrorist** group Islamic State, or IS, who seized territory in Iraq and Syria in the early 2010s. This group believes in a very extreme version of Islam, and it does not speak for the majority of Muslims who live peacefully around the world.

BREAKING NEWS

The Abbasids have introduced a position called a **vizier**, or "chief advisor." This official (below, left) will help run the government of Islamic states. Previously, only high-ranking families have held such power. Now even a male slave can become a vizier if he has enough talent. Perhaps viziers will become more powerful than the sultans one day!

IN THE HAREM

- ☞ Keep out!
- ☞ Family only!

The **harem** (below) was the living quarters of the sultan and his family. Harems were large because a sultan often had many wives and secondary wives, or concubines. The sultan's children also lived there, and many servants. The harem at the Topkapi Palace had more than 300 rooms.

My Medieval Journal

Imagine you are the ruler of an Islamic country. Write a job advertisement to recruit a vizier. List the qualities you think would be useful in an individual who would be able to organize both the government and the running of your household affairs.

Islamic Rulers

The caliphs ruled the whole Islamic Empire. Over centuries, caliphs came from dynasties based in different parts of the Middle East and Central Asia.

Holy Shrine

The Umayyad caliph Abd al-Malik built the Dome of the Rock shrine in Jerusalem in 691. It remains one of Islam's holiest sites.

WHO LEADS ISLAM?

+ Sunnis vs Shia

+ A bitter split

When Muhammad died in 632, his followers argued about who should replace him as leader of the *umma* (community of Muslims). One group believed that only Muhammad's relatives should succeed him. They are now known as the Shia Muslims. The other, larger, group argued that it was not necessary to be a blood relative. They are the Sunni Muslims. The two groups still oppose one another today.

EXPANSION UNDER THE UMAYYADS

✦ Caliphate based in Syria

In 661, Muawiya ibn Abi Sufyan became caliph. He started the tradition of handing the caliphate down through a family, founding the Umayyad dynasty. From their capital in Damascus, Syria (above), the Umayyads ruled until 750. They expanded the Islamic Empire greatly. In the late 600s, the Umayyad ruler Abd al-Malik ibn Marwan made Arabic the official language of the empire.

NEWS FROM AFAR

In 750, the Abbasids seized power from the Umayyads. They set up a capital at Baghdad (left), which became the most important city in the world. The fifth Abbasid caliph, Harun al-Rashid, inspired a cultural boom. Artists, scientists, and scholars made great advances in medicine, astronomy, law, and other fields. The Abbasid dynasty flourished for 500 years.

RIVALS TO THE ABBASIDS

- A Shia dynasty
- Fatimids rule North Africa

The Fatimids were Shia from North Africa. They descended from Muhammad's daughter, Fatima, and his cousin, Ali. The Fatimids challenged the Abbasids right to rule the Islamic Empire. In 909, the Fatimid **imam** Ubayd Allah al-Mahdi (left) declared himself caliph in Tunisia in North Africa. Within a century, the Fatimids also controlled Egypt and part of Syria.

Did you know?

Chess began in India around the 500s, and soon spread to Persia. When the Arabs conquered Persia in 651, they learned the game. From them, it passed to Europe.

A MILITARY DYNASTY

- Descendants of Saladin

Founded by Saladin, a general who fought the Crusaders, the Ayyubids were based in Egypt. They controlled much of the Middle East in the 1100s and 1200s. Saladin retook Jerusalem from the Christians in 1187. The city remained under Muslim rule for the next 800 years. The Ayyubids were great military engineers. They built the citadels in Cairo, Egypt, and Aleppo, Syria.

Friends and Enemies

Islamic forces fought to expand the empire, but they also made alliances with their neighbors. They needed to do this because the empire's wealth depended on trade.

DEFENDING THE FAITH

+ Christians come to fight

The Crusaders were Christian knights who responded to Pope Urban II's call to fight to free Christians living in Jerusalem and Constantinople from Muslim rule. Many thousands of Europeans joined eight major campaigns (right) in the Holy Land between 1096 and 1291. The Christians set up some states in the Holy Land. The states were soon recaptured by Muslim forces, however.

PEOPLE OF THE STEPPE

✦ Genghis Khan leads the Mongols

In 1219, Genghis Khan, the emperor of the Mongol Empire, invaded the Islamic Empire. Genghis had built the largest empire the world had ever seen. He died in 1227, but the Mongols went on to capture Baghdad and kill the caliph in 1258. Just two years later, the Mongols were defeated and many of them converted to Islam.

RISE OF THE SELJUKS
✦ Central Asians seize Baghdad

The Seljuks were tribes from Central Asia. In the late 900s, they started to move west into the Middle East. At the time, the Islamic Empire was weak. A people called the Buyids effectively ruled the caliphate, although there was still an Abbasid caliph. In 1055, the Seljuks seized the caliphate. They ruled from Baghdad and then from Anatolia (eastern Turkey) during the 1100s and 1200s.

MY MEDIEVAL JOURNAL
Imagine you are a wealthy Venetian merchant during the Crusades. Write a letter to a friend explaining why you think you should continue to trade with Muslims even though your fellow Europeans are fighting them in the Holy Land.

A TRADING EMPIRE
☛ Venice rules the waves
☛ Prefers profits to war

Venetian traders were happy to trade with the Islamic Empire—even when other Europeans were fighting in the Crusades. The Venetians bought rice, sugar, and coffee from Muslim traders. Venice (left) was at the end of the Silk Road—the great trade route from China that crossed through much of the Islamic Empire.

END OF A GREAT EMPIRE
+ Roman Empire in the East...
+ ...overthrown by Ottomans

The Byzantine Empire grew out of the eastern part of the Roman Empire. Its capital was Constantinople (modern-day Istanbul). The empire flourished between 330 and 1453, when Constantinople was captured by the Ottomans. The new rulers liked the order of the Byzantine system. They hired many of the Byzantine clerks, and used many of the old empire's ideas about government and taxation.

Islamic Learning

The early Muslims were great scholars who made huge advances in many areas of learning. In contrast, Europe lagged behind during what is sometimes termed the "Dark Ages."

STUDYING THE SKY

☞ New inventions help

Islamic scholars made great advances in astronomy. They charted the precise positions of the stars. They also developed instruments to enable them to track the movement of planets and stars. One key invention was the **astrolabe** (right), which Persian scholars developed from ancient Greek originals. The astrolabe helped measure the height of a star or planet in the sky. It was also useful for sailors trying to figure out their position at sea.

YOU CAN COUNT ON IT!

+ Al-Khwarizmi crunches the numbers...

+ ...replaces them with letters

Al-Khwarizmi was a mathematician at the House of Wisdom, the academy in Baghdad. He devised a system of numbers based on Hindu numbers from India. This is the same system of 1, 2, 3 which we use today. He also introduced a way of solving equations by using letters instead of numbers. The Latin version of Al-Khwarizimi's name gave us the modern name for this system: algebra. It also led to the computer term "algorithm."

TEACHING THE YOUNG

✦ **Mosques open madrassas...**

✦ **...but only for the smartest**

Madrassas (left) were special high schools for boys run by mosques. Only the best students could join a madrassa. Before they joined, they had to learn the Quran by heart and be able to recite it. Students at madrassas learned subjects such as Islamic law, math, history, and logic. The first madrassa was set up in Egypt in 959 to educate future government officials.

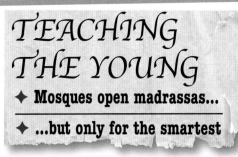

A LITERATE FAITH

☞ **All books valued...**

☞ **...but Quran valued most**

Books were highly valued in Islam. The religion was based on the Quran, which set down the **moral** and religious laws of the faith. Muslims read and learned the Quran. Books were valued both for their discussions of Islam and as records of learning. Skills such as bookbinding, calligraphy, and painting were seen as art forms in their own right. Books were copied by hand, so they were expensive. But advances in paper-making helped to lower prices and make books more widely available.

> " *With no equal on earth ... the most expensive city in area, in importance, in prosperity. ... No one is better educated than their scholars.* "

The 9th century historian and geographer Al-Ya'qubi describes Baghdad under the Abbassids

Islamic Medicine

The early Muslims made huge advances in understanding the human body. They helped lay the foundations of modern medicine.

See!

Eye disease was common, but Muslim doctors were skilled eye surgeons. They were able to remove cataracts from eyes.

MATERIA MEDICA

☛ Medicines from herbs

☛ A specialized trade

Herbs were widely used as medicines. Physicians used an Arabic version of an encyclopedia of herbal cures by the ancient Greek physician Dioscorides. Muslims made potions from plant extracts (right). Official inspectors checked the quality of the drugs. Medicines were usually made from fresh herbs, but dried herbs and seeds were also used and stored in glass bottles to preserve them.

THE CANON OF MEDICINE

+ Ibn Sina's masterwork

Ibn Sina (or Avicenna) was a Persian scholar who wrote a five-volume *The Canon of Medicine*. Based on Greek medical books, the book listed more than 800 drugs, plants, and minerals, and described how to use them to treat sickness and infections. One of the most important of medieval books, it stayed in use until the 1500s. Among his other works, Ibn Sina also wrote books about hygiene and **anatomy**.

> *" The outbreak of smallpox is preceded by continuous fever, aching in the back and shivering during sleep…. Excitement, nausea and unrest are more pronounced in measles than in smallpox… "*

Al-Razi (also Rhazes), a Baghdad physician, describes the difference between smallpox and measles around 900.

My Medieval Journal

Imagine you were sick in a medieval Islamic country. Would you prefer to be treated by a traditional doctor who used magic and prayer, or by a modern doctor who gave you a herbal cure? Give reasons for preferring one treatment over the other.

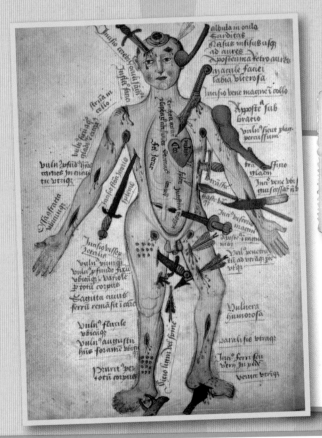

UNDERSTANDING ANATOMY

＋ Learning from Galen

Early Islamic medical books relied on the works of the Greek physician Galen from the 2nd century. Galen had cut open animals to learn about the human body. All the major Arabic medical encyclopedias included Galen's observations. It was only in the late 1300s that an Islamic physician, Mansur ibn Ilyas, published a full anatomical diagram of a human body.

LEARNING FROM THE PAST

✦ **Listen to the Greeks**

✦ **Medicine not magic**

In the early years of Islam, many Arabs still believed that sickness could be cured by prayer or by the use of magic. When the Arabs conquered Persia in the 650s, however, they found medical books by ancient Greeks such as Hippocrates and Galen. The Arabs translated the books into Arabic, and used the ideas of the Greeks to develop a system of medicine based on careful observation and herbal cures.

Islamic Trade

Trade was vital in the Islamic Empire. Merchants traveled widely buying and selling goods, and the empire grew wealthy on their business.

BUYING AND SELLING

+ **Traveling the Silk Road**

+ **Faith travels with goods**

Before Muhammad was born there around 570, Mecca was already a trading center. As Muslim armies conquered territory in Arabia and beyond, Muslim traders (right) opened new trade routes. They traveled east along the Silk Road that carried silk from China, south to North Africa, and west to Europe. Merchants spread Islam as far as Indonesia and Malaysia. Muslim traders brought silk, porcelain, perfume, spices, and slaves to the West.

NEWS FROM AFAR

Islam began in the deserts of Arabia, where **nomadic** peoples used camels to move around. Muslim traders relied on camels to carry goods because the animals could go without water for long periods. For safety, merchants and their animals traveled in groups known as **caravans**. At night, they stayed in a special *caravanserai* (left), an early kind of motel with supplies of food and water.

> " *That desert is haunted by demons ... For there is no visible road or track in these parts, nothing but sand blown hither and thither by the wind. You see hills of sand in one place, and afterward you will see them moved to quite another place.* "

The Islamic traveler Ibn Battuta describes crossing the Sahara Desert in North Africa in the 1300s.

BREAKING NEWS

Everyone knows that Europeans rely on Muslim traders for goods from Asia, such as spices, gold, and porcelain. That's how ports such as Venice, Naples, and Genoa have grown rich. But there are signs things are changing. Now that Europe is emerging from the Dark Ages, more Europeans want to cut out Muslim middlemen and trade directly with the world.

WEALTHY CITIES

- ☞ **Trade generates treasure**
- ☞ **Towns build big**

As the Islamic Empire grew, settlements on major trade routes grew into large cities. Towns such as Constantinople and Samarkand (left) became wealthy. As traders settled in these towns, they built mosques and markets. The markets attracted more merchants, who bought and sold all kinds of goods. Baghdad was the richest of all the trading cities.

Islamic merchants traded a wide range of goods. In Europe, luxury goods from Asia such as silk, porcelain, gold, and spices were in demand. So were many more ordinary goods, including oranges and lemons, which Europeans soon began to grow for themselves. Salt was widely available in Arabia but was more valuable in Africa. Muslim merchants in Africa traded salt for ivory, nuts, gold, and slaves.

WHAT GOES WHERE?

- ✦ **A market for luxuries...**
- ✦ **...and for basics**

Art and Architecture

Islamic artists and architects developed a unique style. They celebrated beauty, but observed religious rules such as a ban on portraying human figures.

Did you know?

The holiest mosque in the world is the al-Haram Mosque in Mecca. It is built around the Kaaba, a building which contains a sacred stone. All Muslims pray in the direction of the Kaaba.

BUILDINGS FOR WORSHIP

+ **Greek features...**

+ **...with an Islamic twist**

At the heart of every Muslim town was the mosque, where men prayed up to five times a day. Mosques were built from local materials, including mud in sub-Saharan Africa. Mosques were either open-plan or divided into four *iwans*, or halls. Some were covered by a dome. Architects borrowed features such as domes and pillars from the ancient Greeks and Romans. They developed the tall minarets attached to the mosques themselves.

BREAKING NEWS

If you want to capture an Islamic feeling at home, try ceramic tiles. Tiles decorated with **geometric** patterns, flowers, and writing decorated many Islamic buildings. Artists learned to cover large areas of walls and floors with colorful tiles that fit together to make larger images (right). The use of tiles reached its peak in Ottoman Turkey.

DOMES AND MINARETS

☞ **Smart engineering...**

The Ottomans built many domed mosques, with a rounded roof covering a large space where prayers are held. The most famous domed mosques are Hagia Sophia (left) in Constantinople (now Istanbul) and the Dome of the Rock in Jerusalem. All mosques have at least one minaret, usually in the shape of tall, narrow columns. Five times a day, a muezzin climbs the minaret to call Muslims to prayer.

> " *Allah is beautiful and he loves beauty.* "
>
> **The Quran**

ART ON PAPER

✦ **Handwriting the top skill**

✦ **Paintings done in miniature**

Calligraphy, or beautiful writing, was an important art for Muslims. Muslims believed that the words of the Quran should be written as beautifully as possible. Calligraphy also appears on buildings and other objects. Miniature painting was another highly prized skill.

COOL WATER

+ **Cooling gardens**

+ **Symbols of Paradise**

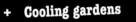

For Muslims, water was a symbol of Paradise, so it was important in Islamic architecture. Buildings often had a courtyard with fountains for cooling (right). Islamic gardens were seen as models of Paradise. They included pools and other water features.

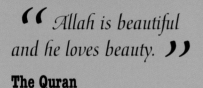

The Spread of Islam

The early spread of Islam across the world was carried out by Arab armies. Later, Muslim merchants traveled widely in Asia and Africa, and spread the faith.

Palace

In the 1300s, the Nasrid dynasty built the Alhambra, a palace in Granada, Spain. Its name means "red palace," for the color of its stone.

INTERNATIONAL EXCHANGE

- **+ Islamic influence spreads**
- **+ Enemies become friends**

As the Islamic Empire expanded, Muslims adopted new ideas they found. They also passed on ideas to the West. From Muslims, Westerners learned to make light cotton clothes, to support buildings with pointed arches, and even to play games such as chess (right). As well, crusaders in the Holy Land took back to Europe the Islamic habit of bathing regularly.

ISLAMIC SPAIN

- **✦ Islam arrives from Morocco**
- **✦ Inspires cultural flowering**

Islam reached Europe when Muslims from Morocco invaded Spain in the early 700s. They set up an empire that lasted until the 1400s. Cordoba and Seville became centers of Islamic culture. In Cordoba, the Great Mosque (left) had 850 pillars supporting a spectacular ceiling. It stood as a symbol of Muslim power in Spain.

HOME FROM HOME

✦ **Islam in North Africa**

✦ **From one desert to another**

By 750, Islam had spread across North Africa from Egypt to Morocco. North Africa resembled Arabia—it had large deserts with little water—but it had many valuable trading goods, such as slaves and ivory. In the 1000s, a group of Arabian tribes, the Banu Hilal, moved to North Africa and settled there.

My Medieval Journal

Imagine you are a scholar at the House of Wisdom in Baghdad. Write a letter to a friend explaining why it might be useful to cooperate with scholars from other religions. How might it help your studies to meet people from other backgrounds?

BREAKING NEWS

Muslim traders traveled across the Sahara to set up trading towns in Africa. Timbuktu and Djenné in Mali were centers of Islamic learning in the 1300s. Timbuktu's library drew scholars from around the Islamic world, while Djenné (right) was a key port on the Niger River.

ISLAM IN ASIA

☛ **Mughals rule India...**

☛ **...lay roots of modern country**

Muslims arrived in India in the 600s, but reached the peak of their power from the 1500s to the 1800s under the Mughal dynasty. The arts flourished under the Mughal emperors such as Akbar (left), who ruled from 1556 to 1605. He set up an efficient **bureaucracy**, which is still in use today.

The Islamic Legacy

During the Golden Age, Islamic scholars, scientists, and artists made advances in learning that would influence and shape the world for centuries to come.

Did you know?

Muslim farmers in Spain used **irrigation** to grow crops such as olives, grains, and sugarcane, even in the dry lands of al-Andalus.

INSPIRING THE RENAISSANCE

✦ Islam's Golden Age...

✦ ...inspires another in Europe

The Islamic Empire constantly embraced the ideas of other civilizations, such as reviving interest in Greek medicine and philosophy. The Islamic Golden Age took place 600 years before the **Renaissance** began in Europe. When the European Renaissance began, it was Islamic scholarship that enabled Europeans to access classical texts, scientific ideas, and philosophy.

WORLD VIEW

+ A shift of focus

+ Europe looks west

A change came as Europe left the Dark Ages behind in the 1400s. A seafarer from Portugal named Vasco da Gama found a sea route to India and the Spice Islands of modern-day Indonesia. Europeans could now deal directly with Asian traders, and cut out Muslim merchants. As well, Europeans reached America in 1492. With a new world to explore, falling trade, and modernization, Europe slowly began to leave the Islamic world behind.

NEWS FROM AFAR

Islamic scholars used classical texts to develop an understanding of the world. They drew remarkably accurate maps, such as this map of Europe and Africa (right, with south at the top). When such Islamic works reached Europe, they gave Europeans a far greater idea of the world beyond their own continent.

THE RECONQUISTA

☛ Get out of Spain!

☛ Christian rulers lead campaign

From around 1000, the Muslims started to lose control in Spain. They lost a series of battles (left) until by 1250 they only controlled the area around Granada. Spain's Christian rulers, Ferdinand and Isabella, finally drove the Muslims out of Spain in 1492 and reunited the country. This completed what is known as the Reconquista, or Reconquest.

LIVING TOGETHER

+ Cooperation between faiths...

+ ...but not for too long!

For centuries, Muslims allowed the people it conquered to follow their own religion. The Muslims made non-Muslims pay higher taxes, but otherwise they were equal. In al-Andalus, Muslims lived side by side with Christians and Jews. The cultures became mixed through intermarriage. After the Reconquista, however, such **tolerance** was rare.

Glossary

anatomy The bodily structure of humans or animals

astrolabe A device for measuring the height of heavenly bodies above the horizon

astronomy The study of stars and other heavenly bodies

bureaucracy A system of officials who make decisions related to government

caliph The main spiritual and civil leader of all Muslims

caliphate The area governed by a caliph

calligraphy Decorative handwriting

caravans Groups of merchants and their animals traveling together

classical Related to the civilizations of ancient Greece and Rome

Crusades A series of religious wars fought between Christians and Muslims for control of the Holy Land

cultural Relating to the ideas and beliefs of a society

dynasty A family of rulers who hand their title from generation to generation

geometric Having regular lines and shapes

harem The private quarters of a sultan and his family

imam The person who leads prayers in a mosque

irrigation Artificially watering land to grow crops

minarets Tall, thin towers on mosques

mosque A Muslim place of worship

moral Concerned with right and wrong behavior

muezzin A man who calls Muslims to prayer at a mosque

mystic Someone who seeks to become one with a god

nomads People without a fixed home

nomadic Wandering without a fixed home

philosophers People who study ideas about life and thought

pilgrims People who travel to sacred places for religious reasons

Renaissance A period in Europeon history of high artistic and cultural development

sacred Very holy

spiritual Relating to the human spirit rather than to the body or physical things

terrorist Someone who uses illegal violence to try to achieve political aims

tolerance The willingness to accept beliefs that are different from one's own

sultans Muslim kings

viceroy Someone who rules on behalf of a king or queen

vizier A high official in Muslim government

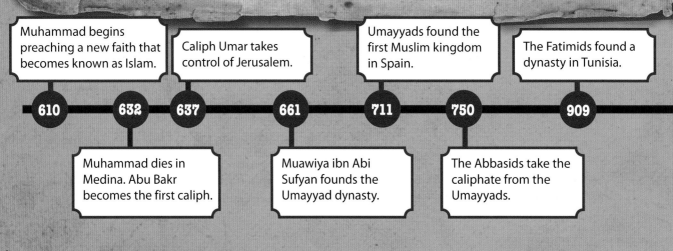

Muhammad begins preaching a new faith that becomes known as Islam.

Caliph Umar takes control of Jerusalem.

Umayyads found the first Muslim kingdom in Spain.

The Fatimids found a dynasty in Tunisia.

610   632   637   661   711   750   909

Muhammad dies in Medina. Abu Bakr becomes the first caliph.

Muawiya ibn Abi Sufyan founds the Umayyad dynasty.

The Abbasids take the caliphate from the Umayyads.

On the Web

www.kidspast.com/world-history/0171-islam.php
This site is full of information about the history of Islam in the Middle Ages.

www.ducksters.com/history/islam/
This website has many links to pages about Islam and the medieval caliphates.

www.historyforkids.net/the-crusade.html
Go to this site to learn more about the Crusades.

www.bbc.co.uk/bitesize/ks3/history/the_wider_world/medieval_islamic_world/revision/1/
Visit the BBC History website to learn more about the Islamic world in the Middle Ages.

Books

Cohn, Jessica. *The Medieval Islamic World: Conflict and Conquest* (Social Studies Readers). Teacher Created Materials, 2013.

Flatt, Lizann. *Early Islamic Empires* (Life in the Early Islamic World). Crabtree, 2011.

Flatt, Lizann. *Arts and Culture in the Early Islamic World* (Life in the Early Islamic World). Crabtree, 2012.

Lassieur, Allison. *Trade and Commerce in the Early Islamic World* (Life in the Early Islamic World). Crabtree, 2011.

Nardo, Don. *The Islamic Empire* (World History Series). Lucent Books, 2011.

Romanek, Trudee. *Science, Medicine, and Math in the Early Islamic World* (Life in the Early Islamic World). Crabtree, 2011.

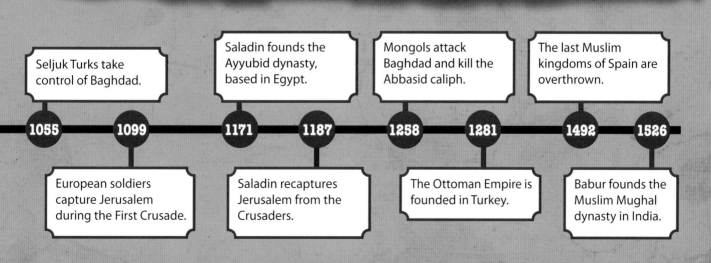

1055 — Seljuk Turks take control of Baghdad.

1099 — European soldiers capture Jerusalem during the First Crusade.

1171 — Saladin founds the Ayyubid dynasty, based in Egypt.

1187 — Saladin recaptures Jerusalem from the Crusaders.

1258 — Mongols attack Baghdad and kill the Abbasid caliph.

1281 — The Ottoman Empire is founded in Turkey.

1492 — The last Muslim kingdoms of Spain are overthrown.

1526 — Babur founds the Muslim Mughal dynasty in India.

Index